D1277569

THE BITE ME SCHOOL OF MANAGEMENT

SCHOOL OF MANAGEMENT

Taking a Bite Out of Conventional Thinking

Kim Shepherd *with* Joanna Sherriff

THE BITE ME SCHOOL OF MANAGEMENT
Taking a Bite Out of Conventional Thinking

Decision Toolbox All rights reserved.
Published by Decision Toolbox Press
Copyright ©2010 Decision Toolbox

Telephone: 562.472.0721
Email: info@dtoolbox.com

www.dtoolbox.com/biteme

Cover and Interior design: Toolbox Creative, www.ToolboxCreative.com
Cover photography by Katie Clark Studios of Laguna Beach, California.

Library of Congress Cataloguing-in-Publications Data
Library of Congress Control Number: 2010935643
Kim Shepard
Joanna Sherriff
The Bite Me School of Management: Taking a Bite Out of Conventional Thinking
ISBN: 978-0-9829798-0-8
Library of Congress subject headings:
   1. Leadership   2. Employee Motivation   3. Success in Business United States

2010

DECISION TOOLBOX
unconventional scalable recruiting

"It is not the critic who counts; not the man who points out how the strong man stumbles, or where the doer of deeds could have done them better. The credit belongs to the man who is actually in the arena, whose face is marred by dust and sweat and blood, who strives valiantly; who errs and comes short again and again; because there is not effort without error and shortcomings; but who does actually strive to do the deed; who knows the great enthusiasm, the great devotion, who spends himself in a worthy cause, who at the best knows in the end the triumph of high achievement and who at the worst, if he fails, at least he fails while daring greatly. So that his place shall never be with those cold and timid souls who know neither victory nor defeat."

Theodore Roosevelt

Acknowledgments

To my Business Partner, Jay Barnett, who has joined me in the arena for both victory and defeat and we managed to hug through both. He is the heart and soul of Decision Toolbox. To Joanna Sherriff, who somehow makes sense of my half-baked concepts and is pure talent at the tender age of 34. To Loren Miner, for actually running the business, leaving me more time for thinking and less time doing and for her stead-fast integrity. Finally to my Mother, Bobbi, for teaching me to dream big, live large, get small, and treat everyone as an equal. If I could give her ANYTHING in this world, it would be a mere one tenth of what she's given me!

Contents

Foreword

Charles Kettering said, "If you have always done it that way, it is probably wrong."

I hope the title *The Bite Me School of Management* got your attention, but I must insert a disclaimer: this will not be a lesson on corporate tough love and whip-cracking micromanagement; in fact, quite the opposite. The intent is to take a bite out of conventional thought and so-called "wisdom" that too many business managers and entrepreneurs have wrongly adopted over the years. Times have changed dramatically and so should the way we run our companies.

We are no longer living in our parents' past where top-down management reigned and employees remained loyal to one company their entire lives. Rapidly changing technology and an unquenchable thirst for advancement, acknowledgement, work-life balance, quality of life, and a green planet has created a "Me Inc." world, and this unconventional shift requires unconventional thinking.

Let me begin by admitting that this book was written in one week in Queenstown, New Zealand, far from ordinary distractions, familiarity, and the luxury of time to continually rework the written word. Instead, all focus was on sharing stories of unusual problem solving, team building, and shared vision in easily digestible sound bites.

My path to leadership has been unusual, to say the least. Coming from a single-parent home where my mother was tasked with having to raise four children alone (me being the oldest), we moved around a lot. In fact, I went to nine elementary schools and three separate third grades. At that point, you either become an introvert or extrovert. I chose the latter and excelled at making friends quickly. Since it was certain that my stay at any given school would be short-lived, I had to quickly assess who would make the best friends and allies. This is where I began to live the concept of attracting more bees with honey than vinegar—a state of mind that serves me well today with my employees, peers, and clients.

Years later, I would choose to become a television reporter where I spent ten years with various networks as a feature journalist. Covering nearly one thousand TV stories, I had anywhere from three days to three weeks (or even three months) to boil the essence of the story down to a three-minute segment for public consumption. Reporting was where I learned the fine art of knowing your audience, a mandatory trait for being not just a successful but also a respected entrepreneur.

Taking what I thought would be a temporary break from broadcasting, I accepted a job (if you can call it that) as a Director of Entertainment for Club Med. I was called upon to assess the guests at any given resort and determine what form of entertainment would best resonate. A production of *The Rocky Horror Picture Show* might not quite fly with a group of tourists from France, much the same way that *Moulin Rouge* would not be the best choice for visitors from New York. Here, I was taught the importance of looking at the big picture first. Sort of like building an entertainment-based business plan.

In 1990, I changed careers again. This time, I entered the field of recruitment with the goal of learning how corporations work from the ground up. Never having worked "inside" a company, my original plan was to start my education from the people side of business and then assess where I might best fit within an organization.

The firm I chose provided engineers for power plants across the country. I didn't know the difference between a mechanical and an electrical engineer and to be honest, didn't really care. About three weeks into this new career, I noticed that an occupational therapist friend of mine was getting constant calls from hospitals and rehab centers with enormous salary offers. I went to my boss and asked for permission to focus on therapy, a bit of an unusual request to say the least.

To me, the math was simple: this was a hot need that recruiters had not yet discovered. Besides, I found therapists to be a lot easier to talk with. One year later, my little healthcare division was more profitable than the company's core engineering offering. In fact, the company name was changed from Power & Electronics Personnel to P&E Search to help disguise the fact that a healthcare division was sitting in the middle of an engineering firm.

In 2000, after building and selling several recruitment-based companies, fate brought me to the most perfect business partner, with whom I would hone many of the stories I'm about to share. Jay Barnett is a true visionary who had always been on the leading edge of his field. In 1992, he founded Decision Toolbox, a small recruitment company that brought Recruitment Process Outsourcing (RPO) (similar to Business Process Outsourcing, or BPO) concepts to the market *before* the market demanded it.

Mine was a history of building large teams of aggressive recruiters; Jay's was in building tools, technology, and processes. Our business backgrounds were a natural fit. But perhaps more important, we were aligned philosophically as well. We wanted to build a company with a heart and soul in an industry renowned for being hugely competitive and for having more than its fair share of junkyard dogs. Recruitment, after all, is an unregulated industry with no curriculum and very few rules. To make things worse, recruitment usually falls under the umbrella of Human Resources. HR is designed to deal with the "what is," where recruitment dwells in the world of "what isn't." The two have little in common except that they both interact with human capital: people, or the lack thereof.

Like many other CEOs, I continually wear many different hats. The trick is to know which one to put on, and when. This can be particularly difficult when you run a virtual company offering a virtual service, with employees (many of them stay-at-home-moms) working from home offices from New Zealand to New Hampshire and all points in between.

Over the past 18 years, I've learned there is a great divide between management and leadership. That divide is the difference between being reactive and proactive and the difference between good and great. The single most difficult challenge facing the leaders of today is the acceptance and mastery of change. The old adage "If it ain't broke, don't fix it" keeps us from creating the vision needed to lead our people and our companies to greatness.

In closing, I would like to share this story, one that is closest to my heart and best illustrates what I hoped Decision Toolbox could accomplish. One of DT's leadership mantras is to never accept a manager's pat on the back or great client satisfaction survey without then saying: "Thanks, but what could I have done better?" By "dwelling in the negative" we are continually uncovering ways to improve ourselves and our company. Thank you to Nicole Cox, our Director of Recruitment, for sharing this story, and for inspiring her team with her words:

This Sunday we scooped up the kids and the dog to go to Holy Jim Canyon. For those who aren't familiar, it's a little dirt road that leads to an unexpected creek. The creek has vines to swing from and rocks to climb. Ever since my son was 10 we've let him drive on the dirt road. Austyn is now 14 and has driven quite a bit. This time my husband let Austyn drive from Holy Jim Canyon onto the pavement all the way to Cooks Corner (that's a couple of miles for those not familiar with the area). Well, you could tell my son was nervous and shocked that he was allowed to do this. He did very well. We stopped and got into our usual seats. I told him that he had done a great job and that I was very proud of him. He watched his rearview mirror, he watched the street signs, he asked smart questions, etc. The very next thing out of his mouth was, "Thanks, Mom, but what could I have done better?"

I'm proud of our company ethics and philosophy. I'm passionate about the way we do business! I'm thrilled that my son has learned to put his ego aside and ask this question early in life. Part of that is due to the lessons I learn from working with all of you. The fact that you ask your clients this question makes you the best of the best.

A Parable

A chicken and a pig were strolling down a street passing several coffee shops with signs that read:

Ham & Eggs $5.99

The chicken looks to the pig and says: "I don't get it, how come you always get top billing?"

The pig replied, "Because, my friend, yours is a contribution and mine is a commitment."

PART 1

DON'T CHEW — SWALLOW YOUR CULTURE

Most entrepreneurs meticulously build their business plans, organizational charts, and boards of directors and assume that the culture will follow. In reality, it is the reverse. A visionary creates the culture and assembles the company around it. It is an art rather than a science, and can be counterintuitive.

Research from the Corporate Executive Board has shown that emotional factors are four times as significant as rational factors when it comes to the amount of effort employees put into their work. The feelings of being "fired up" or "burned out" are emotional states.

So what is culture? Culture is the heart and soul of your vision—it is what you want your baby to grow up to be. And this doesn't mean how big or how much—it is what your company will *mean* to the people who work with you. When work has meaning, people have passion, and when people are passionate they become more than "workers"—they become a committed, unstoppable force.

To raise this healthy, happy, productive child, you have to be a parent who nurtures and rewards as often as you set and reinforce rules. This means getting hands-on, and devoting an abundance of time to selecting your leadership team, ensuring that each person is not only smarter than you in their area of experience, but is committed to your vision.

To illustrate, consider Abraham Lincoln's reaction to the suggestion that General Ulysses S. Grant—unpopular and reputedly a heavy drinker—should be removed from command, to which Lincoln replied:

> *"I can't spare this man; he fights!... If I knew what brand of whiskey he drinks, I would send a barrel or so to some other generals."*

General Grant shared Lincoln's commitment—win at all costs—and as a results-oriented Commander in Chief, Lincoln was willing to buck both popular opinion and the advice of his aides. Ultimately, he would fire five generals during the Civil War, one of them twice (McClellan), in an effort to find men as passionately committed to his vision as he was. In the end, it won Lincoln the war.

Where Lincoln wasn't afraid to hire and fire until his winning culture was built, I recommend developing "colonels with potential" as an alternate, more rewarding process.

> *If your actions inspire others to dream more, learn more, do more and become more, you are a leader.*
> John Quincy Adams

The best executive is the one who has sense enough to pick good men to do what he wants done, and self-restraint to keep from meddling with them while they do it.

Theodore Roosevelt

"Colonels with Potential"

I rarely hire generals. I hire people with *potential,* preferring energy and enthusiasm over experience any day. In the 1990s, I was a senior leader at a healthcare services company, South Coast Rehab Services, and I built an entire team of 40+ recruiters with people from a wide variety of backgrounds—but none from recruiting. Despite their lack of related experience, this team became one of my highest performing teams ever.

South Coast Rehab Services put therapists into skilled nursing facilities (SNF), making it a staffing company that looked like a healthcare company: we put therapists into SNFs, they touch a patient, we bill Medicare, and we make money. The more therapists touching patients, the more money we made, and therefore our growth and success was directly tied to our ability to recruit therapists better than the competition.

I joined the company as VP of Recruitment, and my task was to hire, train, and lead the team of recruiters who would find the therapists we needed to help our company grow. Instead of the conventional approach of hiring based on experience, I decided to hire based on the "X Factor." All I did was open my eyes and anyone I ran into during my day —the exceptional waitress, the efficient sales person at Nordstrom—I offered the chance to realize the potential they plainly possessed. Almost all accepted and some failed, but overwhelmingly, this team came to work every day with a hunger to grow. I just gave them a goal, empowered them to reach it, and got the hell out of their way. To give you an idea of how ferociously they pursued their goals, consider that their nickname around the office was 'Kim's Piranhas' and our CEO once observed that they "ate nails for breakfast."

I could share a million "team spirit" stories from this team, from the daily afternoon conga line, to the birthday gong, to the cross-dressing transvestite (a story for another book), but what best drives home their collective spirit is the bottom line. Remembering that the company's growth engine was our ability to hire therapists, South Coast Rehab Services grew from a $3M company to a $100M company in just three years.

When It's Time to Make a General

Convention dictates a fairly straightforward process for promoting managers. I wonder why an event that is so rich with emotion and energy needs to be confined to a one-on-one, stage-managed exchange. I borrow a bit of Hollywood drama to get every last ounce of leverage out of my promotions.

Consider a typical promotion:

Big Boss calls Colonel Callie into her office, says: *Callie, you've done a great job over the past four years and I am so pleased with your progress as a leader.*

Colonel Callie nods knowingly.

I'm offering you a promotion from colonel to general. Congratulations, you've earned it.

Callie smiles, delivers a short, rehearsed speech about how grateful she is that her hard work was recognized and how much she looks forward to the challenge of being a general. She returns to her desk. Big Boss emails the team to let them know that Callie's new title is General.

Callie might be happy, but by containing this positive energy to just two people, you've missed an opportunity to impact the culture of the entire group.

Several years ago at Decision Toolbox, I had two exceptional colonels who were ready to be promoted to general. Rather than channel conventional ideas, I took quite a different path.

It was Christmas time and prior to our monthly team meeting, our employees had requested business cards for the first time. Once at the All-Staff, I played Santa Claus and surprised the group with new business cards, all in bright red boxes. Holding them to last, I slide the final two boxes to my colonels. Both protested that they had plenty of business cards already, to which I replied: "Open it. You don't have *these* business cards." The Director of Finance opened her box to discover she had been promoted to COO, and the Director of Creative Services learned she had been promoted to VP of Creative Services. The room overflowed the applause and recognition for these newly minted generals and the energy became electric.

No dialogue before, no private meetings, and the entire team got to witness the promotion in real time. Instead if generating a moment of excitement with one person, the whole company got to participate. That's creating exponential energy.

Exponential Energy

Let me give you another example of how you can expand your corporate wealth exponentially. This is on an individual basis, but unconventional nonetheless.

It was in 1995. I was with a small company and had just been promoted from a manager role to a leadership position. In addition to my title, I left behind my monthly bonus checks and was installed on the senior performance pay plan. I remember this meant a sharp decrease in my monthly income, but I trusted that I was making a smart move. Months went by, and all of my foot soldiers continued to earn (and celebrate) big bonuses, and when I didn't, I began to feel unnerved and cheated.

Then I got my first taste of unconventional leadership. I was not pulled into an office, or talked to by a peer or superior, but simply received a generic email stating that my first leadership bonus was coming. I remember calling my mother and saying, "Mom, I think I might get a ten thousand dollar bonus!" and my mom cautioning me about thinking too big and being disappointed. I still fantasized that maybe it is $10K—and could be as much as $20K. About three days went by and I was about to take a weekend trip to Mexico, when I went to the ATM to pull out some cash. I was glancing over my receipt when I let out a yell that caused my friend to start speed-dialing 911. My receipt showed an extra *$100,000* sitting in my ATM account.

My manager could have told me more about what to expect, and the email notification could have contained an exact amount. Instead, my manager knew that by surprising me, she would get even more leverage from an already spectacular reward. She was able to generate exponential energy from a one-on-one event. This certainly wasn't the only big bonus I have received in my career, but it is the most memorable. In fact, I remember every detail, including what I was wearing that day at the ATM.

> *The leaders who work most effectively, it seems to me, never say "I." And that's not because they have trained themselves not to say "I." They don't think "I." They think "we"; they think "team." They understand their job to be to make the team function. They accept responsibility and don't sidestep it, but "we" gets the credit. This is what creates trust, what enables you to get the task done.*
>
> Peter Drucker

Flipping the Hierarchy

Personally I rarely meet a smart person who wasn't smarter than the person he or she reported to—so why give them a boss? I prefer to empower my managers to be their own toughest critic and to provide them with mentors. I've found that, once empowered, star performers are naturally inclined to micromanage themselves and only look outward for leadership, not daily instruction.

A simple manifestation of this approach is our vacation policy at Decision Toolbox. In short, we don't have one. When an employee wants to take a day off, she has two responsibilities: tell management what days she'll be gone and arrange for someone to cover her desk. There is no asking for permission or forms to fill out, and in five years of having this policy, no one has abused it.

Another way of flipping the hierarchy I learned from a good friend of mine, Dr. Izzy Justice, a recognized expert in emotional intelligence (EQ) and a leader in this growing field. Izzy's company, EQ Mentor, practices a meeting format that fosters this same spirit of equal empowerment. At the close of every team meeting, he goes around the table, allowing each person to share one key take-away. As the individual lessons are shared, the administrative assistant is given equal time and footing with the CEO, placing everyone in the meeting on the same level. Simple, but so effective.

The Drunk and the Lamppost

While we are on the subject of meetings, I am reminded of a favorite quote that never fails to inspire me to keep meetings on task:

Most managers use meetings the way a drunk uses a lamppost: less for illumination, more for support.

> *There are five fundamental qualities that make every team great: communication, trust, collective responsibility, caring and pride. I like to think of each as a separate finger on the fist. Any one individually is important. But all of them together are unbeatable.*
>
> Coach Mike Krzyzewski

Cultural Glue

Flipping the hierarchy and exponential energy are both ways to cement your corporate culture. I call it creating "cultural glue." Creating corporate glue is a challenge for every leader, and it can make a good team great, and hold the team together through tough times.

Here is how one of our recruiters at Decision Toolbox describes our glue:

> *Leaving my job at [a Fortune 100 company] to join Decision Toolbox was the scariest decision of my adult life. I was well established and had great pay, benefits, and a retirement plan. What made the decision to move to DT easy for me was when I heard someone say that you should surround yourself*

with people who want you to be successful. My prior company is a place that creates an atmosphere of competing to be the best, even with your peers, so basically no one helps each other, no one is nice, and friendships are rare. At DT, everyone helps, congratulates, and welcomes your life, and ultimately I decided that all the benefits in the world could not outweigh the rewards of working in this type of atmosphere!

Tiger Team

The glue at Decision Toolbox is strong, but not permanent, and keeping it in place is a constant focus as a company grows. In the last year alone, we doubled the size of our recruiting team.

"Tiger Team" is a process I learned from Vistage, an executive roundtable group. Whenever a Vistage member has an especially difficult problem, he calls a Tiger Team and the group heads to an off-site meeting where the roundtable spends several hours tackling the problem collectively.

At Decision Toolbox, we have applied the Tiger Team process with two key changes: first, we added a rule that every idea is valid and worthy of exploration; and second, we schedule Tiger Teams ahead of the problem, before it manifests. These modifications ensure that the Tiger Team's energy remains positive—not argumentative or defensive—and that it is a proactive planning session rather than a reactive, emergency intervention.

At a recent All-Staff meeting, we divided the recruiting team into four Tiger Teams and gave them one challenge: tell us what we need in order to preserve DT's glue when we have one hundred recruiters. We had allowed them an unlimited budget, and yet 95 percent of the glue items on the list cost nothing. What they valued was time (and communication) with leadership, recognition for their successes, and support from their peers. In fact, they were vehemently against expensive prizes—no cruises or vacations in Hawaii for top performers—and valued smaller gestures such as manicures and pedicures more highly. This exercise was illuminating on so many levels and I treasure it as a daily reminder of the power and wisdom of collective problem solving.

Green Flag

In the late 1990s I was at the San Diego Zoo at the primate enclosure, and along with about thirty other people I was watching the chimpanzees, mesmerized, as they rhythmically, slowly swung from branch to branch. Some of the older chimps sat on the ground, but everything about them was calm and restful.

Suddenly, out popped a small chimp from a hole in the wall, and he burst onto this peaceful scene screeching and jumping around like his tail was on fire. The crowd was immediately intrigued—what was up with this little guy? Was he hurt? No—he was excited—so excited he was running around the enclosure screaming... and waving something green. As the crowd watched this monkey celebrate, I shouted: "I've got the green thing! I've got the green thing!" As we laughed, the whole crowd was buoyed by the joy this little guy was expressing. It gave me an idea.

The following Monday, I shared this story with the team at DT and handed out a small green flag to everyone. From that point forward, everything worth celebrating at DT became a "Green Flag." Landed a new project? Green Flag! Filled a position? Green Flag!! Great client survey? *Green Flag!!!*

It may sound corny, but the Green Flag creates exponential energy around simple everyday events. Again, a recruiter on our team expressed it best:

> *When I joined DT, I thought the whole Green Flag thing and all of the 'woo-hoos' and hugging was a little silly. Now, I land a project and I can't wait to send out my Green Flag notice. Then, I sit back and wait for all of the congratulations to flow in, my smile getting bigger and bigger. It's the best part of my day.*

Pods

No matter what strategies you put in place, however, at a certain size, team glue starts to break down. To keep things "sticky" at DT, we divided the recruiting team into smaller "pods" of three recruiters each. The smaller the group, the more personalized the interactions, the stickier the glue.

After some initial resistance, new mini-cultures arose in the pods: they gave themselves names, slogans, and even team chants. This part wasn't surprising, but what was unexpected was the degree to which these teams became independent of management and fully capable of solving almost all of their own problems. They became the expert "cockroach hunters."

Cockroach hunting is my affectionate term for identifying and stamping out tactical problems — that is, anything that, left alone, will multiply in importance until it prevents a project from moving forward to successful completion. In recruiting this might be a hiring manager who won't return calls, a lack of qualified candidates for a niche position, or an offer that was declined at the eleventh hour.

Any one of these cockroaches has the potential to throw a project completely off the rails, and a recruiter ignores them at his own peril. But it is human nature to do exactly that: sweep the problem under the rug, deal with it tomorrow, tomorrow, tomorrow, and when the entire project fails because of it, roll out the ready-made excuse: "My hiring manager went AWOL! This opening is impossible to fill — no candidates exist with those qualifications! The client made a crappy offer!"

Cockroach hunting on Pod calls keeps the recruiters on task and focused on solving their problems as a group. In fact, they start the call with a chant: "Today we will find and exterminate our cockroaches!" The energy they create enables them to conquer just about anything they encounter and dramatically reduces the amount of management micro-management required. What follows is a testimonial from another of our recruiters that illustrates both the empowerment and the glue in the Pod:

I was diagnosed with glaucoma at a relatively early age and it was being treated with various medications over a 10-year period. The pressure in my eye was getting out of control last year and was no longer responding to medication. My specialist said that I needed immediate surgery or I would potentially lose my vision in my left eye permanently. Obviously, this was devastating news for me personally, but I was also buried with projects at the time. I barely got the words out of my mouth on my Pod call, and every single team member jumped in to offer their help during my down time which was about to start the very next day. I can't tell you how much relief I felt and how appreciative I was to be part of this incredible team. Because of the brilliance of our system, my project and client history was at everyone's fingertips, so the transition was seamless to my clients. To me this is an example of great leadership. Leadership didn't have to be involved in managing this transition, other than to be kept informed and be supportive.

Sit or Sing

So, you've got your pods formed, the exponential energy is flowing—and along comes a groovebuster I call the "Kiss of Death." Sounds dramatic, I know, but this common mistake has the ability to completely dissolve your cultural glue and extinguish the energy you have worked so hard to build, and it only takes 20 minutes. My bet is that you have already delivered the Kiss of Death several times this week.

Let's set up an example. You lead a team of ten sales people, all of whom are making $60 an hour. Every Monday morning, your team has a scheduled meeting at 9 am and the agenda includes a recap of successes and lessons from last week and goals for this week. So far, so good: we have structure and an action plan.

Then along comes human nature. At 9:00 on Monday morning, one person is sitting at the conference table. At 9:05, two more people arrive, talking about their weekend. Three more arrive at 9:10 with their coffee in hand, and finally, the rest of the team rolls in at 9:15. At 9:21, in comes the boss, excited about the conversation that delayed him and proceeds to share his news with the group. "We've landed that huge new client we've been chasing for weeks! That's why I'm a bit late..."

Sound familiar? Let's assess what really happened from the trench level. Unwittingly, this leader committed four cardinal groovebusters:

1. You reminded your team: I am the boss and you are not empowered to start the meeting until the boss arrives. This is an unintentional "screw you."

2. You embedded the message that the employees' time is not valuable, that it is the boss's time that is the most important.

3. You proved that you are an idiot, because if you take ten people x 20 minutes x $60/hour, you just flushed $200 of productive time down the toilet.

4. Most harmful of all, you punished the only person who showed up on time by wasting 20 minutes of her time.

The good news is: this problem can be solved for $9.99 and a quick trip to Target. Pick up a clock with a second hand, and set a rule that if the "cheek" is not in the "seat" by one second after 9:00 A.M., the tardy arrival will sing a song of the team's choosing. Here is the key: no one is exempt — especially not the boss.

I remember a few years ago being on a conference call trying to close a million-dollar deal. At 8:45 A.M., I started trying to wrap up the conversation for my 9 A.M. All-Staff, but the client still had questions, and despite my attempts, I left the call at 9:02 A.M. — deal in hand, but late to the meeting. As I entered the conference room, my Green Flag celebration died on my lips as I faced a roomful of solemn faces. One of my recruiters pointed to the clock and announced that the team unanimously agreed — I was to sing "She's a Brick House" and only after the song was completed could I celebrate the million-dollar deal.

To this day, everyone on the team can recall the day CEO sang "Shake it down, shake it down down" and also the day our COO gave an emotional rendition of "Somewhere over the Rainbow." I can't remember the last time a staff member has been late to a meeting or called upon to sing.

PART 2

BUILDING AN EMPIRE IN SMALL BITES

I've been blessed to find people who are smarter than I am,
and they help me to execute the vision I have.
Russell Simmons

Minding the Empire

Why is it that all managers complain of not having enough time in the day, while at the same time, these same managers are struggling to ensure that their staff have enough tasks to keep them busy? One of the greatest challenges facing leaders is effective time management, and a caring, supportive culture can further complicate the picture.

For example, at Decision Toolbox, the leadership team "reports" to the employees and we strive for a very "human" and personal relationship with our team members. "Family" is a cliché, so I'll stick with "community" to describe our culture. It is human nature for good managers to want to solve problems for their direct reports, but usually this means taking ownership of the problem and completely relieving the employee of any responsibility.

In taking the employees' problems onboard and making them her own, the leader becomes trapped in the minutiae of day-to-day operations. Much like Alice heading down the rabbit hole, these tactical tasks eat up an entire day—and eventually the entire week—and the leader never has a chance to pause, raise her head, assess, and see the forest for the trees.

There are many parables about time management, but perhaps the simplest and most visual is from Stephen Covey in his book *First Things First*. In it, he shares the following story experienced by one of his associates:

> *I attended a seminar once where the instructor was lecturing on time. At one point, he said, "Okay, time for a quiz." He reached under the table and pulled out a wide-mouthed gallon jar. He set it on the table next to a platter with some fist-sized rocks on it. "How many of these rocks do you think we can get in the jar?" he asked.*
>
> *After we made our guess, he said, "Okay. Let's find out."*
>
> *He set one rock in the jar... then another... then another. I don't remember how many he got in, but he got the jar full. Then he asked, "Is this jar full?" Everyone looked at the rocks and said, "Yes."*
>
> *Then he said, "Ahhh." He reached under the table and pulled out a bucket of gravel. Then he dumped some gravel in*

and shook the jar and the gravel went in all the little spaces left by the big rocks. Then he grinned and said once more, "Is the jar full?"

By this time the class was on to him. "Probably not," we said. "Good!" he replied. He reached under the table and brought out a bucket of sand. He started dumping the sand in and it went into all of the little spaces left by the rocks and the gravel. Once more he looked and said, "Is this jar full?" "No!" we roared.

He said, "Good!" and he grabbed a pitcher of water and began to pour it in. He got something like a quart of water in that jar. Then he said, " Well, what's the point?" Somebody said, "Well, there are gaps, and if you work really hard you can always fit some more things into your life."

"No," he said, "that's not the point. The point is this: If you hadn't put these big rocks in first, would you ever have gotten any of them in?"

At Decision Toolbox, we have applied the "Big Rocks" theory to our process flow, giving our recruiters the smartest and most efficient process. We call it "Inverting the Pyramid." First, let's take a look at standard operating procedure in recruiting. Typically, the process looks like this:

1. A hiring manager has an opening. He sends urgent notice to HR that this position needs to be filled yesterday

2. HR leaps into action and advertises the position immediately on the appropriate job boards, using the job description on file

3. HR receives hundreds (sometimes thousands) of resumes and begins sifting through them for candidates to send to the hiring manager

4. The hiring manager reviews the resumes and tells the recruiter what's missing, and the recruiter begins a second, recalibrated round of screening

Sound familiar? There are three glaring problems with this process that have applications across an organization. Leaders should watch for them and stamp them out like cockroaches.

First, HR launched its process without a clear sense of the desired outcome. It makes perfect sense in hindsight. HR should have downloaded from the manager exactly what he was looking for, why he has looking for it, and how to find it. But it is amazing how often we fall into the trap of simply following an established process rather than doing what makes the most sense.

Second, and without a clear strategy to dictate action steps, HR launched a "shotgun" approach rather than a strategic "sniper" campaign. By using a canned job description—about as interesting and easy to read as a tax return and something that was never intended to be an advertisement—the shotgun approach simply blasts an incomplete and unimpressive message to a wide audience. Talk about a wasted opportunity.

Finally, critical time is wasted in the most important stage—selection. Every project or initiative has its "rubber meets the road" stage and in recruitment it is candidate selection. Great candidates have a very short shelf life and hate to have their time wasted.

> *If I only had an hour to chop down a tree, I would spend the first 45 minutes sharpening my axe.*
> Abraham Lincoln

Design what you want...
...or deal with what you get

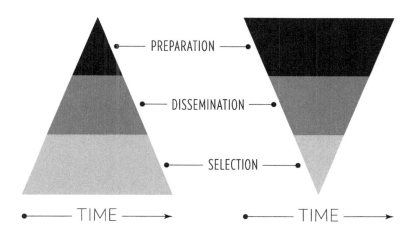

Inverting the pyramid means investing more time on the front end of the process to save time on the back end, or, in other words, "Design what you want, or deal with what you get." Staying with the recruiting example, the pyramid (see graphic below) on the left illustrates a search where a generic ad is placed, which generates a landslide of generic resumes, which results in hours of wasted time sifting through them to identify top talent.

The pyramid on the right illustrates that extra time spent in the preparation stage of each recruitment search (i.e. developing your advertising and marketing campaign) will reduce the overall *number* of resumes received but improve their *quality*, and thus reduce time spent screening and selecting a hire.

Naturally, your company's culture is a big rock, and remember that it needs constant attention and nurturing, applying this same strategic approach.

A Word About Competition

Healthy competition is the lifeblood of a company, and the most productive company cultures are structured to challenge every team member to run faster and jump higher every day. However, competition can also destroy culture faster than you can say "team building exercise."

Teams, Trouble, and Triage

Back in my days as VP of Recruitment for South Coast Rehab services, I built a high performance team in an unconventional manner. What is today an amazing business success story—we grew from a $3M company to a $100M company in just three years—was almost cut short by a complete culture collapse. Let me explain.

Being new as a visionary, I drank my own Kool-Aid when we hit $40M in revenues. In just a few short years, South Coast had grown almost 1000 percent, primarily on the backs of my recruiters. We were the darlings of the company; well, darlings who ate nails for breakfast. Around this time, I vividly remember attending a weekend leadership retreat in Palm Springs where I spent the weekend back-slapping and drinking in the accolades for building such an amazing, cohesive, productive team.

Still riding this high, I walked into the office at 9:00 on Monday morning only to be cornered in my office by my two line managers. My fearless leaders were actually physically jostling each other, arguing about who had the right to talk first about the problems on her team. Apparently, not only had the team fallen apart, but their leaders were broken as well.

Seemingly overnight, the team had transformed into a group of highly competitive individual athletes looking to best each other, rather than themselves. Gone was the teamwork, high-fives, group brainstorming, and crackling creative energy. Instead, we had all of the classic corporate, political behaviors: cliques with in-fighting, chest thumping at team meetings, and intense lobbying for prime projects quickly followed by sabotage from the losing camps. It was chaos.

Looking at my two line managers arguing and taking a quick inventory of all sharp objects within their easy reach, I was struck with the irony—and the enormousness—of my situation. Not 12 hours earlier, I had been sitting at the leadership team bragging about my team and its revenue numbers. Back in the real world, I realized that I had blinked and missed it: the team was broken and needed to be rebuilt from the ground up.

The first thing I did was ease past my lady wrestlers into the cubicle space. At 10:00 am, I assembled the team, told them to go home for the day, but instructed them to return at 8:00 am the next day in their pajamas with their favorite pillow. Since they were acting like children, we were going to tackle our problem from that perspective.

When the team arrived back on Tuesday morning in their favorite jammies, they were greeted with graham crackers and little cartons of milk. At lunch, we dined on peanut butter and jelly sandwiches and juice in sippy cups. Everyone was instructed to drop a business card in a big fish bowl. I declared a state of emergency.[1] We were in the healthcare business and we were hemorrhaging. Nothing short of the Red Cross was going to save us. The "Red Cross" solution was a complete re-structure of the department into four sub-teams: triage (rapid fills with high turnover), ICU (challenging projects in need of special care), rehab (ailing projects that need to be brought back on track), and hospice (projects offering little hope of a favorable outcome, but still needing care).

Naturally, everyone was scared, and everyone wanted to work triage or rehab and no one wanted ICU or hospice, but the difference was that now the competition was structured and directed. To further dilute individual rivalry, each team rotated members so that by the time four months had passed, everyone had competed against everyone else, and everyone had been on the same team together. The team spirit and glue were reborn.

For me, this was a painful and humbling lesson to continually check the "health" of the culture, and that it can fall apart when you least expect it.

> *Management is efficiency in climbing the ladder of success; leadership determines whether the ladder is leaning against the right wall.*
>
> Stephen R. Covey

Putting Your Ladder Against the Right Wall

There is a difference between a task, a goal, and a vision, but leaders often confuse them. As an illustration, I was involved in a goal-setting exercise with a CEO roundtable group, and one CEO—a highly accomplished professional and leader of a large company—listed one of her Big Rocks as "joining a yoga class." My reaction was, "Great! I'll drive you to the class tomorrow. So now let's list your goals!"

Additionally, many leaders' goals are quickly forgotten when the business climate turns sour. There's nothing like an economic downtown, rising energy prices, or exploding healthcare costs to re-order a leader's priorities. While there isn't a good time to de-emphasize culture—as my competition story illustrates—if there is a worst possible time, it is during a business downturn. To keep culture as a Big Rock and relevant, a downturn is the time to look at individual battles that can be won instead of the war.

I remember giving a keynote speech a few years ago to a room full of nurse recruiters. My challenge was daunting—with a national shortage of 200,000 nurses, nurse recruitment was about as much fun as root-canal —and looking out at the mood of the crowd (best described as desperate bordering on catatonic) I realized I needed to get creative quickly. After a brief introduction, I took a quick temperature check and asked: "How many of you feel like it is an impossibility to fill your current nurse openings?" Every single hand in the room went up. Oh boy. So I picked one recruiter out and asked: "How many nurses do you need? And she replied "Fifty", and then I asked her how many she already had on staff, and got the response "Two hundred." I posed the question again and recruiter number two answered: "I have one hundred fifty but I need twenty-five more—and I've been trying to fill them for a year."

After a pregnant pause I challenged the group with the thought that there wasn't a shortage of nurses—I just had to teach recruiter number one to steal fifty nurses from recruiter number two. To accomplish this, recruiter one doesn't have to be perfect, just slightly better than the competition. Understanding and exploiting the chinks in the competitor's armor requires a sniper strategy rather than the shotgun approach these recruiters were applying.

I had a similar experience when giving a speech to the California Bankers Association where business was being crippled by a shortage of tellers. Instead of my planned speech about recruitment trends and best practices, I spent an hour dissecting teller recruitment and helping the attendees develop individual teller recruitment strategies.

In both of these examples, these managers had become so focused on the war that they had lost sight of the battle. This is the role of the leader—to keep the team focused on winning individual battles and not let the size or weight of a Big Rock become overwhelming.

> *You will never "find" time for anything. If you want time, you must make it.*
> Charles Bruxton

Egg Timer

Some days, being the visionary is harder than others, and if I don't live every day by design, I end up losing focus—and lost battles aren't too far behind. I've solved this problem with a $3 egg timer. My theory is that anyone can sprint for 45 minutes, no matter how distasteful the task at hand. Except for the rare long-distance runner who can grind it out all day, most of us cannot focus for extended periods and still be highly productive.

It must sound simplistic, but it is powerful. For any unstructured time in my day, I take one of my Big Rocks and list a series of tasks related to it. Sometimes my Big Rock is driving sales; sometimes it is to simply be the visionary. Then, I set my egg timer for 45 minutes and spend that time completing as many tasks as possible. When the buzzer goes off, I take a break—I have some coffee, go for a quick walk, phone a friend—and then prepare for my next 45-minute sprint. By spending my minutes in a structured manner, I use my day by design and keep my focus where it needs to be: on my Big Rocks.

Leading by design is a constant theme of this book. It is human nature to look backwards for lessons rather than forward for inspiration, but much like cockroach hunting keeps managers on task to solve problems, every leader needs to find his or her visionary zone to maintain focus on tomorrow, next week, next month, next year...

> *Leaders need to be optimists. Their vision is*
> *beyond the present.*
> Rudy Giuliani

Finding the Zone

I am an avid cyclist. In 2007, I rode my bicycle 600 miles in seven days from San Francisco to Los Angeles to raise money for AIDS awareness. It was during a training ride for this event that I found my visionary zone.

I was peddling through a monotonous, solitary 40-mile training ride in hot, dusty Santiago Canyon where there was nothing to look at but sagebrush in four shades of beige. I was reduced to looking at the lines in the road when I suddenly fell into a zone. I suddenly had a vision of Decision Toolbox as a cabin made of Lincoln Logs where I could clearly see each part: the leadership team, revenue generators, support staff, sales, finance, operations, A/P, and A/R. As I looked at this cabin from all sides, I had the sudden realization that the base of this cabin was expanding rapidly (we had enjoyed 50 percent growth year over year for the past three years), and the roof—the leadership team—was being stretched to the point that it was about to collapse.

With no distractions and where no one could reach me, I was able to pull the cabin apart and put it back together piece by piece. When I was finished, I discovered that there were some key pieces missing, including critical components such as an expanded business development function and a quality department.

Many CEOs feel that once the Board of Directors says "good job", their visionary duties are discharged. Not so. As a visionary CEO, I visit my zone at least once a quarter to pull the business apart and put it back together.

In Microtrends, *Mark Penn reports that 4.2 million Americans now work exclusively from home (a nearly 100% increase from 1990), while some 20 million do it part time.*

> *Work is something you do, not someplace you go.*
> Woody Leonhard

Going Virtual

Finding "work-life balance" is one of the most abused clichés in business today. Why? Because there is no such thing as work-life balance in corporate America today. Conventional corporate structures don't allow for balance, just the illusion of working towards it.

Instead, I have eliminated the word "work" altogether and strive for "life balance." I've only got one shot at this life, so I try not to compartmentalize, aim to become more efficient, and leverage technology to blend my work and my life. This does **not** mean my work has become my entire life. It means I have reinvented myself as a leader of a virtual company.

Leaping Off the Virtual Cliff

At my CEO roundtables, all too often I listen to leaders who are perfectly positioned to transform their company into a virtual one to great financial gain, but who are afraid to take the first step. These same CEOs sit in their corner offices and email the COO in the next-door office and call their VP of Sales rather than walking down the hall. What they don't realize is that *this is virtual work*, and the only hurdle that needs to be overcome is ego. Ego prevents leaders from accepting that the company can function without its leaders—especially it's CEO—as a physical presence.

I fully sympathize with this hesitation as I was in love with the virtual concept long before I implemented it. In fact, my partner Jay Barnett and I only took the leap when we were physically pushed by the threat of bankruptcy.

In 2000, I joined Decision Toolbox as president, and Jay and I led the company on a rapid growth clip. In just over eighteen months, we were on track to double in size. Then along came September 11. Overnight, just about every company went into a hiring freeze and massive layoffs dominated the news. Not a good time to be in recruitment. About 65 percent of our competitors went out of business during this time; it was our industry's version of the Great Depression.

Jay and I remain fiercely proud of DT's status as a privately held, self-funded company, and rather than throw in the towel, we brought in a turnaround consultant to show us the path out. He drew up 27 action steps to save the company, and every single one looked impossible. Among the most painful was letting go of several key staff members who had been loyal and committed to Decision Toolbox.

Another was abandoning our Class A office space in Long Beach, California, which had been designed and decorated by Jay and Debra Barnett with great love. It was much more than an office; at the time, it seemed like the very heart of Decision Toolbox and to close it down would mean the end of our company—and our dream. Fortunately, our financial consultant was on hand to coldly point out that, actually, *staying* in the office space would mean the end of Decision Toolbox, so we moved out.

It was gut-wrenching, but the scars of those days have well and truly healed. Today, Decision Toolbox has zero office space and over fifty team members. In 2008 and 2009, we were listed among Inc.com's fastest-growing privately held companies. In 2009, we were very proud to learn that Decision Toolbox has been named a winner of the 2009 Alfred P. Sloan Award for Business Excellence in Workplace Flexibility[1], distinguishing the company as a leading practitioner of workplace flexibility and effectiveness in Long Beach and across the nation.

The flexible work environment at Decision Toolbox goes beyond work-from-home options: the entire company is virtual and all of its team members work from home offices. Sophisticated, proprietary technology coupled with technologies such as VoIP phones, IM, and social networking tools keep the team linked together, while a progressive, results-focused management style keeps performance and productivity at a high level. The company has team members throughout Southern California and in Atlanta, Concord (NH), Dallas, Portland, Seattle, Washington DC, and even in New Zealand.

The glue that holds the company together is technology (Jay's Recruiting Machine) and our unconventional culture. Our

---

1. The Alfred P. Sloan Awards for Business Excellence in Workplace Flexibility are part of the When Work Works project, an ongoing initiative of Families and Work Institute, the Institute for a Competitive Workforce (an affiliate of the U.S. Chamber of Commerce), and the Twiga Foundation. Through When Work Works, these organizations provide research, resources, and recognition to employers nationwide, and share the results of research on creating effective and flexible workplaces that meet the needs of the 21st century.

experience hitting rock bottom helped us to open our eyes (and keep them open!) to new ideas, no matter how outrageous or impossible they might seem.

Getting into a suit, commuting hours to work, spending time at the water cooler, "earning" two weeks of vacation time each year, requesting time off to tend to a sick child — technology has antiquated all of these conventional ideas.

Your leap into the virtual world doesn't have to be dramatic; simply start with using it just one day a week, and monitor not only the productivity but the health of your culture.

The Business Benefits of Going Virtual

1. *Reduced real estate expenses:* IBM saves 40 to 60 percent per site annually by eliminating offices for all employees except those who truly need them. Others estimate the savings at $2 for every $1 invested.

2. *Increased productivity:* Internal IBM studies show gains of 15 to 40 percent. USWest reported that the productivity of its virtual employees increased, some by as much as 40 percent.

3. *Higher profits:* Hewlett-Packard doubled revenue per salesperson after moving its sales people to virtual workplace arrangements.

4. *Improved customer service:* Andersen Consulting found that its consultants spent 25 percent more time face-to-face with customers when they did not have permanent offices.

5. Environmental benefits: A U. S. government study showed that if 20,000 federal workers could telecommute just one day a week, they would save over two million commuting miles, 102,000 gallons of gasoline, and 81,600 pounds of carbon dioxide emissions each week. The emissions savings for one week under this arrangement are equivalent to the amount of carbon dioxide produced by the average car over 9.3 years.

The man who views the world at 50 the same as he did at 20 has wasted 30 years of his life.
Muhammad Ali

Mascara Management

One fun time (and life!) management trick I have implemented in my virtual workday is something I call "mascara management" (or, "shaving management" for the men). It has come to mean "Kim's mental health management" but it is primarily another way I use my day by design.

To get ready for an in-person meeting takes me at least an hour and a half of hair, makeup, dressing, etc. After spending approximately 20 percent of my working life in "prep" mode, I decided to spend that 20 percent more wisely and made a rule: I never put on mascara for one appointment and every week I carve out one "mascara free" day.

A mascara-free day is a day to attack my Big Rocks list, burn through my call list, and everything else I've been itching to get done while sitting in my car on the freeway.

USA Today has come out with a new survey: Apparently three out of four people make up 75 percent of the population.
David Letterman

Managing Efficiencies

One of the unconscious obstacles that prevent leaders from taking the virtual plunge is that a virtual company requires leaders to be masters at managing efficiencies. Most companies focus on managing people; in a virtual company, you manage *process* and lead people.

Identifying your Key Performance Indicators, also known as KPIs or Key Success Indicators, is the essential first step in managing efficiencies. I have three rules for developing KPIs: first, the number has to mean something. Letterman's quote above is one of my personal favorites for that very reason—so many leaders devote hours to tracking, reporting, and analyzing numbers that have no meaning. Second, a KPI should reflect your goals as a company, and third, it has to be quantifiable.

As leaders, we have been taught over the years that micromanagement is a bad thing, and from the top down, it is. But if you empower your managers to lead, they will innately micromanage themselves. You just have to hire the right people to begin with.

PART 3

GOBBLE UP AN UNFAIR SHARE OF THE WORLD'S TALENT

I hire people brighter than me and then I get out of their way.
Lee Iacocca

Getting Your Unfair Share of the World's Talent

Every leader lists hiring great talent as a Big Rock, but almost every company I've worked with wrestles with how to make this a reality rather than an empty refrain. Changing times make this an increasingly difficult task.

The U.S. economy—and therefore the U.S. talent market—is experiencing one of the greatest upheavals in its history, rendering "business as usual" outmoded. Understanding these changes and how they will affect your workforce is essential in obtaining your unfair share of the world's talent.

Across the centuries, revolutions have been speeding up and heating up: the Agricultural Revolution stretched across 150 years; the Industrial Revolution lasted a mere 90 years in comparison, and it took Silicon Valley just seven years to reinvent the way the world does business. And if technology has forever changed the way we look at time, our next, Stealth Revolution, will forever change the way we look at matter.

Imagine the impact of a technology revolution that will create seven million new jobs within the next few years, including some 300 new position types, the likes of which have never been seen before. Then consider that the companies doing the hiring will be introducing products that might, for example, cure cancer, make crude oil obsolete, or even re-engineer humans to become resistant to disease, increase strength, and improve intelligence. Who cares about creating a killer new app when saving the human race is an option?

This is the "next big thing": the nanotech revolution. Nanotechnology is the ability to understand and control matter at the nanoscale or about 1 to 100 nanometers. (One nanometer is one billionth of a meter. A sheet of paper is 100-thousand nanometers thick.) Very soon, nanotech companies will explode onto the scene: economists predict the market for nanotech products will reach $1 trillion by 2015 in the U.S. alone, so they'll have plenty of dollars to throw at new hires as well. If you don't think your company could go one round, let alone ten, with this kind of opponent in the war for talent, the future is about to steal your workforce.

Just to bring it a little closer to home, consider that every other baby girl born today will live to see age 100. In the year 2012, we could be eating genetically altered bananas that could repair the cartilage in our knee. By 2018, experts predict that brain enhancement chips will be available to enhance our children's mental horsepower 35 percent. (Think of what this will do to affirmative action: how many brain-enhanced children do you allow per school?)

Or, consider another similar "stealth" product that hit the shelves in 2008. Take a drive down to your local Rite Aid pharmacy, and there, next to the pregnancy, H.I.V., and cholesterol test kits, you'll find a DNA test kit. Released in March 2008, the Identigene DNA Paternity Test Collection Kit is the first to be sold through a major pharmacy chain. Over-the-counter DNA testing has some fairly huge consequences (just ask the kid who just found out that "Uncle Dave" is actually "Daddy") but its arrival created minimal buzz.

Times are indeed changing, and soon we might need a brain enhancement chip just to keep up. The key to competitive hiring in changing times is understanding your talent pool.

New Ideas Gen Y is Bringing With Them

1. *Me-Inc Mindset:* This is a free-agent generation. They are willing to pay their dues if they're learning and advancing, but will not be held back.

2. *Work-life Balance:* Especially important for Gen Y, who value flexibility in their lives. This includes work

schedules, telecommuting, home-office arrangements, and dress code.

3. *Social Conscience:* This generation expects to make a difference, and they want their employers to help them contribute as well. According to the 2007 Volunteer IMPACT survey by Deloitte & Touche USA LLP, Gen Yers "prefer to work for companies that give them opportunities to contribute their talents to nonprofit organizations."

4. *Demand for Feedback:* Gen Y expects feedback and validation often, and particularly values mentoring.

If you pick the right people and give them the opportunity to spread their wings — and put compensation as a carrier behind it — you almost don't have to manage them.
Jack Welch

Me Inc.

Our employees are no longer our employees — they are entrepreneurs who choose to reside under our roof (or virtual umbrella). It is a Me Inc. world.

Generation Y: born between 1977 and 1995

We Baby Boomers have a tendency to think Generation Yers are fly-by-night, spoiled, hedonistic little brats. But consider that there are 79 million Gen Yers and they outnumber Baby Boomers, and that *Fortune* magazine predicts Gen Y may be the "most high-performing workforce" ever. We're old, they're young, and we need a dose of their energy, rather than burdening them with our apathy.

Recently I was working with a client who had identified an extremely talented young manager—a Gen Yer—whom she wanted to hire. She was about to put this superstar candidate through a lengthy interview process. The problem was this superstar was interviewing with three other companies as well as the client's. If the hiring manager had followed her standard practice—interviewing on Monday, reviewing on Tuesday, discussions with peers on Wednesday, and circling back with the candidate the following Monday—the candidate was certain to take another job offer. Instead, I recommended that she send a text message immediately following the Monday interview that read: "Thanks for your time. We think you are a superstar and we want to make a place for you on our team."

The manager continued to communicate with the candidate in this way, and ultimately, the superstar turned down a higher salary offer to join her team. When asked why, the candidate replied: "Not one of the other companies I interviewed with connected with me on this level. They thought I was all about the money, and sure that's part of it, but only a small part. There is so much more."

As leaders, we tend to look at younger people as being less qualified, less dedicated, and less everything—all of which is a bad thing. But let's flip it—Gen Y will bring new thinking into your company. Where Baby Boomers are just now accepting work-life balance, green planet, and technology, Gen Yers are already wired that way. They were born with it.

So when managing or interviewing Gen Yers, remember their priorities and talk to them like a human being—"I know you have a choice—I know you have options. What would you like to know about me?" Take a proactive lead and this will set you apart from the competition.

> *Hire people who are better than you are, then leave them to get on with it…; Look for people who will aim for the remarkable, who will not settle for the routine.*
> David Ogilvy

Suitors and Sifters

The job market follows the same laws of supply and demand: sometimes you have exceptional candidates banging your door down, and other times you're hiring Grade B beef because it is all you can find.

Visionary leaders develop two strategies, one for each extreme of the job market spectrum: job rich/candidate poor and job poor/candidate rich. With a plan in place for both contingencies, managers can stop worrying about the economy and start hiring by design. This isn't a new idea—it is just common sense. If you think back 65 years, there was a forward-looking group of hiring managers who did something similar…

Consider this recruitment challenge: you just filled two million positions with hard-to-find (no—impossible to find) talent. You're feeling pretty good. Now you find out you need to fill *two million more* in half the time. And the candidates not only

Mike Public

notes:

MetLife
MetLife Auto & Home®

Call
for

aren't looking for new jobs, they've never had jobs. And, if you don't fill them, the entire U.S. economy could shut down.

Where am I? I'm talking about February 1943, when the United States had 13 million women employed and needed to hire two million more within 12 months in order to keep the country and its industry functioning.

Rosie the Riveter was created for what became the most successful advertising recruitment campaign in American history. She helped to hire more than two million women, almost all of whom had never worked outside their own home. Rosie was on posters, postage stamps, and even had her own song. There were 125 million ads placed with her image: Womanpower ads, most of which were full pages, were among the pages of almost all major magazines of the day. Motion pictures, newspapers, radio, trade press, employee publications, and in-store displays all tied in to the universal rallying cry.

With Rosie the Riveter, these hiring managers defied the odds—and convention—to become the ultimate suitors.

Impossible is just a big word thrown around by small men who find it easier to live the world they've been given than to explore the power they have to change it. Impossible is not a fact. It's an opinion. Impossible is not a declaration. It's a dare. Impossible is potential. Impossible is temporary. Impossible is nothing.

Muhammad Ali

Black Holes and Orks

Just as important as building an internal culture of respect among your employees is fostering a culture of respect within your hiring process.

No matter what size your company is, technology has enabled you to reach hundreds, thousands, and even hundreds of thousands of job seekers with every opening you advertise. Since you can only hire a tiny percentage of the candidates you touch, this process generates exponential rejection. It doesn't have to: you can't hire everyone, but you can leave every candidate with a positive experience.

Businesses historically treat job seekers with contempt by asking them to complete lengthy application forms and then allow "we'll contact you if you are a fit for our requirements." Of course, 99.9 percent of applicants never hear from the company again, and their hour of invested time just fell into an uncaring black hole.

Job seekers have a long memory, and one resentful applicant in 2008 could be the star candidate who declines your offer in 2010. On the other hand, something as simple as a courteous "Thank you for your interest in our company but this position is now filled" could earn entrance into a rich referral network somewhere in the future. If every step in your hiring process expresses respect for the job seeker's time and interest, you can transform these interactions into *positive* exponential energy.

Sometimes, there just isn't enough talent to go around. I mentioned in the foreword that this book is being written in New Zealand and recently I had an opportunity to meet and talk with Miranda Rivers, the extras casting director for the *Lord of the Rings* trilogy, some of which was shot within 10 miles of where we are writing this book.

Miranda's task was to hire 5,000 people to play 20,000 roles in difficult conditions (heavy makeup and costumes, 16+ hour days, often in inclement weather) for just $70 a day. In some cases, she cast entire towns as extras. What grabbed my attention was hearing her talk about casting the orks—those huge, frightening creatures that lived underground. As you would expect, Miranda cast tall men to play the orks, but right when filming was scheduled to start, lambing season arrived on the South Island of New Zealand.

Overnight, Miranda's "orks" vanished back to their farms and the director was left with primarily women. Eyeing her 5'2" replacements, she did what any unconventional leader would do: didn't panic and got creative—fast. To see if her idea was a success, rent *The Lord of the Rings* and see if you can tell which orks are men, and which are women. Bet you can't.

Building Your Bench

It's inevitable: you stumble across a great asset to your team at a time when there are no openings, no opportunities to offer. What you *can* do when you encounter a candidate you're unable to hire immediately is to show your interest by making a formal offer with a blank start date. Once they are a part of your "virtual bench," open the door to regular communication so that when the day arrives and you have an opening on your team, you can reconnect quickly and the building blocks of a relationship are in place.

Keeping House

A competitive job market also creates great temptation. Not only are hundreds of thousands of new jobs advertised each month, nearly half of employers (49 percent) expect to increase salaries on initial offers to new employees. Talk about the grass being greener.

To counteract temptation—and proactively address turnover—I conduct staged, mock exit interviews with my key talent. I ask them to envision the scenario that would tempt them away from Decision Toolbox, and then use their answers to address any unmet needs. What I have found so far is that most of what they list isn't expensive, and in many cases is free.

A Second Parable

An old Italian man lived alone in New Jersey. He wanted to plant his annual tomato garden, but it was very difficult work, as the ground was hard. His only son, Vincent, who used to help him, was in prison. The old man wrote a letter to his son and described his predicament:

Dear Vincent,
I am feeling pretty sad, because it looks like I won't be able to plant my tomato garden this year. I'm just getting too old to be digging up a garden plot. I know if you were here my troubles would be over. I know you would be happy to dig the plot for me, like in the old days.
Love, Papa

A few days later he received a letter from his son.

Dear Pop,
Don't dig up that garden. That's where the bodies are buried.
Love, Vinnie

At four the next morning, FBI agents and local police arrived and dug up the entire area without finding any bodies. They apologized to the old man and left. That same day the old man received another letter from his son.

Dear Pop,
Go ahead and plant the tomatoes now. That's the best

I could do under the circumstances.

Love you, Vinnie

The only place success comes before work is in the dictionary.
Vince Lombardi

Three Yards and a Cloud of Dust

Great for a laugh, the tomato garden story is actually a perfect illustration of unconventional thinking at its best. Sales is another area of business that has been drowned in consultants, seminars, books, lectures, programs, and essays, and I can see why. I find it is the most difficult of all departments to build and manage. Many times, leaders become so tangled up in our underwear trying to build sales processes, infrastructure, and KPIs that we forget that the sales team is supposed to be selling.

Sometimes, the first steps are the hardest, whether for a new salesperson, or simply during a down business cycle, getting the momentum going is the number one priority. To get the ball rolling, I deploy a strategy I call "three yards and a cloud of dust." For football fans, you know this means grinding it out over four downs to gain 10 yards, and starting again. It might take a while to reach the end zone, but you reach it in the end and have smaller celebrations along the way.

Many organizations are structured more for the Hail Mary pass, which are by design high risk. Remember Vinnie—the ultimate goal is just to get the tomatoes planted. How you get it done doesn't have to be pretty.

PART 4

SUPER-SIZED SALES (WITH OR WITHOUT FRIES)

Having hit a wall, the next logical step is not to bang our heads against it.

Stephen Harper

Sales Quotas and Hitting the Wall

The next level of structure managers impose on sales are quotas. Sales reps "dial for dollars" and aim to make hundreds of calls a day and celebrate if one of those results in a real conversation. But running into 99 "no's" every day is not only de-motivating, it is a huge waste of resources. At Therapy International, we found a way to make ten calls a day and make upwards of 90 percent of them result in a sale.

Taking you back to South Coast Rehab Services again, our specialty was therapists for skilled nursing facilities—but the SNF is just one of ten specialties a therapist can choose, including sports medicine, pediatrics, and traumatic brain injury intensive care. Convention at the time was to purchase licensure lists that included therapists from all specialties, hand these lists to the recruitment team, and have them call their way down the list. These conventional teams were built to run into nine walls before finding one candidate. They were structured to fail.

After running into this wall one time too many, I took a cocktail napkin—and a mighty good margarita and listed the biggest names I could think of. And on that napkin I formed a company called Therapy International. Since I didn't quite know where I was headed yet, I figured that was the one name I couldn't outgrow. I would move my team out of South Coast's corporate offices into our own space, call ourselves "Therapy International," and begin a strategic campaign to find SNF therapists at warp speed.

Instead of the shotgun approach, Therapy International would abandon the licensure lists to the competitors and call into the SNFs with this proposition: "Give me five minutes of your time, and let me be your free agent. Tell me what you would like in your next job and I will only call you back if I can find it." Instantly, we flipped the easy "No, thanks, not interested" hang-up into a positive exchange of priceless information with potential candidates.

Once our recruiters had these profiles in hand, we would then match them up with SNF buildings we had in the area. What made it easy was the fact that our recruiters knew their candidates' "hot buttons"—e.g. we found you a position that offers a $6K raise, has a shorter commute, and put you on the management track you want. We had a near-100 percent fill rate, which was unheard of in our industry. We hired nearly 2,000 therapists and to this day, no one has replicated this simple strategy.

> *The only real voyage of discovery consists not in seeking new landscapes but in having new eyes.*
> Marcel Proust

Sea Lion Sales Approach to Territory Domination

The same cut-to-the-chase mentality brings us to our next sales strategy. Over the years, I have sat on many CEO round-tables and listened to many CEOs talk of elaborate plans for market penetration, the hiring of exorbitantly priced con-sultants to build this strategy, and analyzing their elaborate approach *ad nauseum.*

Sometimes these strategies are years in the making. But I prefer an easier path (perhaps perceived as less intelligent, but then again, the concept of this book is "Bite Me" to con-vention). At Decision Toolbox, a management Tiger Team envisioned a local territory domination strategy, so rather than spending hundreds of hours on Hoovers.com or hiring pricey consultants, I got in the car. I drove down the freeway, made a note of every company name I saw, and that became our target list. We landed some 50 percent of these clients, some of the most highly visible companies in our local market. Territory domination is a perception, both in your own mind and in the minds of your prospects: if you can see the signage, and that's a client of DT's, then DT owns the territory.

Here is where the sea lion comes in: on my way to meetings, I love looking up at the building and seeing our client name, chanting out "Ars, ars, ars (ours, ours, ours)."

> *When all think alike, then no one is thinking.*
> Walter Lippman

Channel Partners

In 2006, I gave a keynote speech at the Newspaper Association of America's national conference in Chicago. During the speech, I spoke to a group of managers who have seen their revenues shrink by over 50 percent in recent years. Guessing that recruiting talent wasn't going to be at the top of their priority list, I instead gave them a speed lesson in the recruiting industry and how the newspaper business can build a new river of cash through channel partnerships. Instead of viewing recruiting companies as competitors—we compete for a share of the same Human Resources budgets—align yourselves with them to offer your clients a more complete service—a *solution.*

A Channel Partner is a person or a company with a complementary service, who is knocking on the same doors as you, and who is *connected.* I don't mean that they are on LinkedIn, attend networking groups, and talk a big game. I mean *connected* to the degree that when she tells a member of her network to jump, that member says "How high?" Rather than viewing him as a potential competitor, view him as a partner with direct influence over your prospect list. Isn't that someone you want on your team?

With a little bit of structure and ingenuity, you can supplement your sales efforts by leveraging channel partnerships. At Decision Toolbox, we have Channel Partners who are previous clients, major corporations, and some of the most respected consultants in the human capital space. Compensation doesn't have to be complicated, either. Just take what you would normally spend on a sales lead, and give that to the Channel Partner in the form of a revenue share.

The most important rule is to feel *good* about any dollars that go to a Channel Partner. I remember during one leadership meeting at Decision Toolbox, our Operations Manager brought it to our attention that we were writing $80,000 in Channel Partner checks that month and what were we going to do about that? My response was: *FANTASTIC!* Writing lots of Channel Partner checks is the right kind of problem to have—it is not a fixed cost and it means business is coming in. Win-win!

The challenge for the person at the head of this initiative—which is currently my role—is that you have to accept that you will kiss a lot of toads before you meet a prince. Much like any sales organization, you are going to run into three types of people: hunters, gatherers, and vegans. You're familiar with hunters and gatherers, but when meeting Channel Partners, you'll also run into people who really just want to go out to lunch and talk, go out to dinner and talk, meet for coffee and talk. They have the potential to waste big chunks of my time, so I classify them as "vegans" for being so low in calories. Good Channel Partners are hunters with a "protein-rich" diet of connections.

Unfortunately, it is almost impossible to classify a Channel Partner until you have some time invested, but I have never felt that any time spent with a potential Channel Partner is wasted. Some Channel Partners I had flagged as vegans after several lunches and no leads actually turned into "octopuses," or a "hub" Channel Partner who introduced me to eight other potential partners. I take a long-term view to the time I invest, and know that every now and then, I will meet an octopus in an unexpected place.

The final word on Channel Partners is in keeping with my overarching message on glue. For a Channel Partner to be a long-term asset to your company, wrap them up in your culture as much as possible. At Decision Toolbox, we give our Channel Partners customized web portals where they can log on and instantly see their pipeline and upcoming payments. We also invite them to our All-Staff meetings for a dose of the DT Kool-Aid, as well as our annual holiday networking party for a bigger, more elaborate "thank you."

> *Do what you do so well that they will want to see it again*
> *and bring their friends.*
> Walt Disney

Warm Washcloth Story

Recruiting can be an ugly, disheartening place. In this industry, we work with human nature on both sides of our service delivery equation, and that leaves us with twice as many opportunities for failure through factors we cannot totally control.

Despite the ugliness, Decision Toolbox has built its reputation on service. Our clients don't just like us — they love us — and are more like converts than customers. An approach that has helped us develop our reputation is what we refer to as the "warm washcloth."

In Jeffrey Gitomer's book *Customer Satisfaction is Worthless; Customer Loyalty is Priceless* he tells the story of how delighted he was to receive a warm washcloth upon check-in at a Hawaiian hotel. His delight was amplified by the *unexpected* nature of this simple, thoughtful gesture.

We have applied the warm washcloth theory in as many aspects of our service as possible, but haven't limited ourselves to the customer experience. At a recent All-Staff meeting, we gave our employees the warm washcloth treatment and aimed to appreciate them at every turn. It was a richly rewarding day, but some of the highlights included a welcoming greeting from a manager along with a single rose, a full buffet breakfast, a copy of the day's paper (which happened to feature a cover story on Decision Toolbox in the business section!) at every seat, a champagne toast and a surprise guest speaker — Tim Hart, CEO of Leading CEOs. Finally, and perhaps the most surprising and best remembered, we had a massage therapist onsite who, every 30 minutes, tapped a team member on the shoulder for a 20-minute massage.

Admittedly, we took the warm washcloth to the extreme in this example, but the recruiters saw the meaning that simple, surprising gestures could have. Now, as often as I hear "I've got a Green Flag!" I also hear "I just warm-washclothed my client!"

> *People don't want a quarter-inch drill, they want a quarter-inch hole.*
> Theodore Levitt

Selling the Drill or the Hole

Surprising your customers with a warm washcloth is a fun and rewarding *satisfaction* strategy, but to truly keep your customers *loyal*, you have to be delivering *solutions*.

Ted Levitt's famous quote is a great illustration of what I mean; your client doesn't want a product; she wants the solution. Typically, sales people (me included) talk far more than we listen in order to uncover a prospect's hidden needs. Instead, we should spend 90 percent of our time asking questions to find out what is the solution the prospect wants, and then 10 percent of the time explaining how what we're selling delivers that solution. It's about being valuable.

> *If you make customers unhappy in the real world, they might each tell six friends. If you make customers unhappy on the Internet, they can each tell 6,000 friends.*
> Jeff Bezos

Staying in the Negative: Thank you, but...

Another deceptively simple philosophy that has exponential power is a willingness to "stay in the negative" when receiving feedback. As a general rule, people want to please. We would far rather say to our waiter: "Yes, thank you, everything is fine" than admit that our "rare" steak actually resembles shoe leather. It takes far more strength to be confrontational and send the dish back than it does to simply leave the steak and never return to that restaurant.

This avoidance behavior is another kiss of death that requires more than surveys and quality check phone calls to reverse. As an example, I remember a recruiter at Decision Toolbox filling a very high-profile senior leadership role for one of our clients for about $5,000, when he had been paying $100,000 in the past. But when we circled back with this hiring manager nine months later to check in on his hiring needs, he responded with an email asking to be removed from the Decision Toolbox mailing list. Rather than simply acquiesce, Jay Barnett picked up the phone and asked why. It took 15 minutes of probing before the truth was revealed, and it was bad.

Apparently, a candidate we had helped the client to find had turned into a complete nightmare, alienated the entire staff, and had threatened litigation before HR was able to get him out the door. Apparently, the trouble started just weeks after we placed the candidate, and yet the client never once picked up the phone to complain, ask for help with a replacement, or more to the point, ask for his money back. He just didn't plan on ever using our service again.

Our policy at Decision Toolbox is to stay in the negative and probe for real feedback, particularly if it is painful to hear. Whenever a client shares positive feedback, we respond with "Thank you, but we are a work in progress. What can we do better next time?"

On the flip side, sometimes when a client *only* has negative feedback all the time, it's time to fire your customer.

> *I like long walks, especially when they are taken by people who annoy me.*
> Noel Coward

Survivor Immunity Challenge

Every now and then, you come across a client whom you can't seem to please. As a friend of mine once wisely said: "There is a very fine line between a classic car and a piece of shit." Sometimes, the relationship just isn't worth saving.

You're familiar with the TV show "Survivor"? At Decision Toolbox, we instituted the Client Survivor Immunity Challenge after a particularly painful experience. This client had engaged us on several searches, but instead of being a partner, took great pleasure in beating up on our staff, avoiding our invoices, refusing any feedback, and generally putting up roadblocks at every turn.

Upon hearing from my Director of Recruitment for the fourth time in as many weeks, I decided to call a CEO-to-CEO meeting and make one last attempt to get in the negative and turn this relationship around. When her reaction was to launch a fresh attack on my team, I held up my hand and asked her to pause. Then I asked her if she was familiar with "Survivor." When she said yes, I informed her that the DT Tribe had voted, and had voted her off the island. I was Jeff Probst (the host of "Survivor") and I was officially extinguishing her torch. Eyes open wide in surprise, she protested: "You can't do that! I'm the client!" "Exactly," I said.

PART 5

TAKING A BIG BITE OUT OF CHANGE

If you're not making mistakes, you're not taking risks, and that means you're not going anywhere. The key is to make mistakes faster than the competition, so you have more chances to learn and win.

John W. Holt, Jr.

Mastering Change — Staying Proactive

Change is always good. The more change you experience as a leader, the more opportunities you have to learn, leverage, and grow. Most people, however, hate change:

Our dilemma is that we hate change and love it at the same time; what we really want is for things to remain the same but get better.

Sydney J. Harris

As leaders, part of our job is to be prepared so that when the time arrives, we are ready to lead with conviction.

Tsunami Planning

Cataclysms hit businesses every day: the loss of a key client, lawsuits, a public relations nightmare (think Dell's exploding laptops), and sometimes even *gaining* a large new client. When AT&T secured exclusive rights to support Apple's iPhone on its wireless network in 2007, Steve Jobs said he'd be happy if they could grab one percent of the global cell phone market, or about 10 million units for 2008. Instead, Apple sold closer to 43 million—25.1 million in 2009 alone—and acquired 14 percent of the global smartphone market. And AT&T's network simply couldn't handle the traffic. The result? Lots of *very* unhappy customers. Unhappy *vocal* customers who were very savvy to the impact of social networks.

Once a quarter, the DT management team spends a day in my living room envisioning our "What If" scenarios. These "Tsunami Planning" sessions tackle global scenarios that have the potential to completely overwhelm our operations. Recent topics have included: how to respond in the case of a major natural disaster in Southern California, the impact of quadrupling the business overnight, and the loss of a key executive.

While natural disasters and other acts of God remain remote possibilities, if the economic crash of 2008/2009 has taught us anything, it has taught us that the economic cycle is going to remain dynamic, despite what Alan Greenspan thought. So, in early 2008, before everything had really tipped over and recruiting was still booming along, DT was rolling out strategies for growth, while *at the same time* planning for a major reversal in both the job market (our candidate supply) and new business. As a result, DT was able to weather what was a significant hiring downturn, and even roll out new products and services, while several competitors went bankrupt.

The purpose of a Tsunami Planning session is not to come up with what you know, but to explore what you don't know. If you are just going through the motions and listing our action steps, you're not planning for tsunami: it *should* be a painful and difficult process, and the result is peace of mind.

I haven't gotten hit by that proverbial bus yet, but we have a plan for it in case it happens. And that's a good feeling.

EPILOGUE

The Evolution and Devolution of the Corporation

This book pulls apart and analyzes business strategy in small bites, but if you step back and view your company's culture, leadership, hiring & retention, sales and change management strategies as a whole, the culture of most growing companies goes through a predictable and destructive pattern.

A few years back, I was a passenger on the rollercoaster ride from a $3M startup to a $100M corporation. At the time, I thought that the cultural quicksand that we sunk into was exclusively our own making, but after many more years in the business world, I have seen countless other companies go through the same cycle, from Passion, to Profit, to Performance to Protection. My hope is that as your company evolves through these growth stages, you can revisit the "Bite Me School of Management" and if not avoid—find solutions for these common pitfalls.

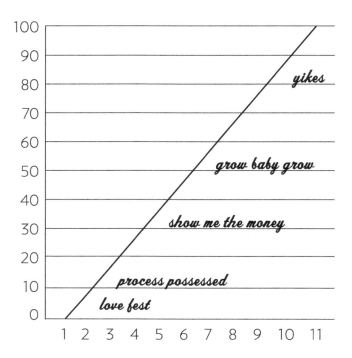

From Passion, To Profit,
To Performance, To Protection

"Passion" and "start-up" go hand in hand. The road to $5M in annual revenue is an incredible, emotional rollercoaster ride of creating something new, along with a crew of people who are on-board, sharing an all hands on deck culture of 'get 'er done.' At its best, $5M can be a love-fest of back-slapping self con-gratulation. And why not. Some 90% of businesses don't make it past the first 12 months of operation. But somewhere around $12M—almost like hitting adolescence—the company begins acting, by necessity or design, a bit more mature and a bit less 'seat of its pants'. Passion is tempered by maturity, and with more revenue comes more people, more process, and more responsibility. For me, this was when...

Profit becomes Prophet

At $20M, the corporation has graduated to adulthood and all of the baggage it entails. Suddenly, there are four (or ten?) times as many mouths to feed, intricate when–did–we–build–that processes, customers you've never heard of, suppliers you've never met.

At $30M, we as managers forget our roots. Our feet are no longer in the trenches—we have middle managers for that. Instead of looking at our people, we're now looking at our numbers and "profit" becomes "prophet".

At $40M, we drink our own Kool-Aid and really start to lose touch with our people in a big way. Giddy with the success of building a successful (and money-making!) venture, we feel invincible. A symptom? You catch yourself lecturing to your worker-bees about "commitment" and "hard work" and "building value".

At $50M, we start to get edgy about our financials again. After a period of feeling secure in our cash flow, we've realized that we need outside investors with deep pockets to fuel the next road of growth. In addition to diluting equity, we hand over the reins with rose-colored glasses—until the investors start making their first demands.

From $60M to $100M, the quicksand really starts moving under our feet. Pulled in a million different directions by investors, the board, customers, suppliers, vendors, $60M is when passion—and sometimes integrity—becomes a distant memory. By $80M we're wondering how we can unload this burden on someone else. At $90M, while the board is talking Initial Public Offering (IPO) and acquisition, we're daydreaming about the glory days at $5M when passion was king and work wasn't work.

At every $10M in revenue growth, companies undergo significant cultural changes, many of them slight enough to escape real notice, but over time, they compound to form the quicksand of "corporate" or conventional thinking. Some companies do avoid these pitfalls and become business school case studies, putting the rest of us to shame. But then, how many business school darlings have gone on to become cautionary tales, such as Enron, Toyota and Dell? Exploding laptops anyone? No—no one is immune, and as leaders we're all in the same boat together.

AWARDS & RECOGNITION

Since writing this book, Decision Toolbox has been recognized for its success and leadership by a variety of organizations:

1. Winner of the 2009 Alfred P. Sloan Award for Business Excellence in Workplace Flexibility, distinguishing the employer as a leading practitioner of workplace flexibility and effectiveness.

2. Named to the Inc 5000 annual ranking of the 5000 fastest-growing private companies in the country in 2007 and 2008.

3. Selected by Cisco Systems as the exclusive vendor to provide RPO and specialized and inexpensive recruitment services for Cisco partners in conjunction with the launching of Cisco's Partner Talent Network.

4. Kim Shepherd has been nominated for both the Los Angeles Business Journal and the Orange County Business Journal's prestigious "Women in Business" Awards.

5. Kim Shepherd has been selected as an Advisory Board Member to the American Solutions for Winning the Future: Jobs and Prosperity Task Force. Awarded for dedication for developing real working solutions that will lead to the recovery of the American Economy, awarded by Newt Gingrich, General Chairman.

GLOSSARY

Channel Partner: A "virtual sales force" of people who refer business to Decision Toolbox and receive revenue share for that referral. Some of Decision Toolbox's recruiters are also Channel Partners.

Cockroach Hunting: Big problems that can breed if not squashed by their pod.

Dog with Fleas: This is a project with a problem. At DT, we try to avoid projects that are 'Dogs with Fleas'.

Green Flag: An internal celebration at DT. Team members send a "Green Flag" notification to celebrate something great, e.g. new project opening, a hire, a great quality survey, etc.

Pod: Small teams of recruiters who meet once a week to brainstorm and problem solve regarding their projects.

Pony Bonus: A bonus that DT Team Members receive when a client calls him/her directly to open a new project or specifically requests him/her. To launch the program, DT created a mock-up of a race-track with individual "ponies" for each team member and moved them around the track each time a bonus was earned. The overall winner in the first month of the program also won a trip to the races in Del Mar. The term "pony bonus" stuck.

Tiger Team: A carve-out brainstorming meeting with one topic. The purpose is to spend an hour — or sometimes two — devoted entirely to that topic. Key to the success of a Tiger Team meeting is two primary rules: #1: no team member can "throw-up" on any ideas presented (all ideas are valid during the brainstorming session); and #2: everyone must leave the meeting with clear action steps to move a solution forward.

Tsunami Planning: Imagining a problem before it happens and blue printing the solution, complete with assigned action steps.

Kim Shepherd

joined Decision Toolbox in 2000, bringing her unconventional approach to the company she had previously admired as a client. Calling Kim unconventional is an understatement.

She is a regular speaker at national and regional events on the topic of recruitment best practices, recruitment process outsourcing, leadership vs. management, time management best practices, generational communication (Boomers vs. Gen Y), and corporate culture in a virtual workplace.

Kim is an active member of the Adaptive Business Leaders Executive Roundtable and the National Association for Women Business Owners (Orange County Chapter). She is on the Board of Trustees for Girls Incorporated of Orange County, and is a member of the Orange County United Way's Women's Philanthropy Fund. Decision Toolbox won the 2009 Sloan Award for Business Excellence in Workplace Flexibility for the Long Beach, California area.

Joanna Sherriff has partnered with Kim

Shepherd on countless writing and creative projects during her eleven-year tenure with Decision Toolbox. Joanna's writing has been featured in a variety of publications including the *Harvard Business Review, HR Executive Magazine,* and the *Orange County Register.* She has also developed creative content for Kim Shepherd's national speaking engagements at venues including the National Human Resources Association National Conference, the Newspaper Association of America (NAA) National Recruitment Forum, the Harvard Business School Entrepreneurs Conference, and the National Association of Women Business Owners. Joanna began her writing career with Decision Toolbox, eventually becoming the company's Vice President of Creative Services in 2004. Joanna has a Bachelor's Degree from Connecticut College in New London, Connecticut and an MBA from the Graziadio School of Business and Management at Pepperdine University in Malibu, California. Joanna recently joined Fairfield Caterers Inc. as the Director of Corporate Development, and is in charge of corporate strategy.

CPSIA information can be obtained at www.ICGtesting.com
Printed in the USA
LVOW012348171012

303362LV00004B/1/P